True to the God in You

True to the God in You

Harry Matthews

Harry Art Publishing

First published in this edition December, 2020
by Harry Art Publishing
www.HarryArt.co.uk
England, U.K.

All rights reserved.

© Harry Matthews, 2020

No part of this book may be reproduced, stored or transmitted in any form or by any means whatsoever without the prior written permission of the publishers. This book may not be lent, hired out or resold or otherwise disposed of by way of trade in any form of binding or cover other than that in which it is published, without the prior consent of the publishers.

Typeset and designed in Venice by Harry Art Publishing.
Cover from original oil painting "Pentecostal Fire" by Harry Matthews
© Harry Matthews.
Cover design by Harry Matthews.

First Printing, 2020

A CIP catalogue record for this book is available from the British Library.

ISBN 978-1-8383498-5-1

Contents

Dedication **viii**

1 Preface **1**

2 The Hollow of the Old Packing-case **5**

3 True to the God in You **8**

4 Agony **10**

5 When There Was No Eternity **12**

6 God's Love Shines Brighter **13**

7 When We Changed Our Flocks At Night **15**

8 Nova Testamentum **17**

9 Ambiguous Loss **19**

10 Heavy Fell The Wrath **21**

Contents

11 Elegy for a Degenerate 23

12 The Glade Beyond the Forest 25

13 An Angel Spoke on the Cool Breeze 27

14 Some untimely thought did instigate 30

15 The Angel of Comfort 31

16 Lyric Harmonic on the String of Sensuality 33

17 The Painful Frustrations of the Poet 36

18 Power Divine Taught You to Tend 37

19 He Found the Place 40

20 The Place to Teach (Bite Before Bit?) 42

21 He Taught You How to Find 44

22 Banished From Our Tree of Life 46

23 No One Shall Harm You 48

24 A Heart in Darkness 50

25 The Northern-most Pilgrim 52

26 Let Who Listens Close That door 54

27 Wampish Refrain of Your Whining Obstruction 56

Contents

28 The Quockerwodger 58

29 Escape From The Sluberdegullion Snake 60

30 The Waterfall Where We Once Stood 62

31 The Perverted Belfry 64

32 The Ecclesiastical Survey 66

33 What Carried The Day 68

34 Spin It Clean Off The Reel 70

35 (Un)Cloaked in Mystery 72

36 One By One Hill won 74

37 Bionicle of Falling into Deeper Darkness 76

38 Flowing waves to Rapture 79

39 On the Pleasure of Sunbathing 82

40 On Conversing with Blackbirds 84

41 Haros the Hedgehog 85

42 Footnotes 86

About The Author 93

{ 1 }

Preface

True to the God in You is about self-fulfillment, strength, loyalty, courage and sacrifice. These are the necessary properties of the Trinity of Love: I myself, *You and God*.

If we understand *True to the God in You*, like the preceding works that came to me this year, is the image of that sphere on the cover of the first collection *Sonarification*: The first book is the centre that closes inwards and outwards. The second, *Twynd*, is its radiation from the centre to circumference. The Third book, *Hyperion*, is the summary of the centre, radiation and circumference.

The God, the poet as prophet within his time, and the Holy Fire are the *three-in-one* here depicted on the cover of this sixth book, that arrived by the wilderness of the fourth, *Woodwose*, and shadows of the fifth, *The Lost Shadow of Things*.

The shape, position and effect is an expression of our covenant with God, of His unconditional, unfailing love and mercy. All the contents of the six works return here in their unity, development and fullness. What began as an active core has passed in compelling growth, glowing with in-pouring light of the holy spirit that is the Kingdom of God; His True Church.

These poems are ἐνέργεια, the action and result of superhuman activity, of Imagination and Inspiration, which comes from God. *Enérgeia* (the root of the English term "energy") means "power in action". *Enérgeia* ("divine energy") typically refers to God's energy which transitions the believer from point to point in His plan (accomplishing His definition of progress). It is given as superhuman power in the Bible, whether of God or of the devil; but please let us go with God: **Ephesians 3:7**.

Therein lies the radiant power of this book of poems, just as the earlier books can be described in landscapes and moods, as love poems, in the tone of voice, content, expression, gesture and wisdom. *Twynd*, concerns only two people, and yet it celebrates perceptions of God revealed in nature. *Hyperion* is replete with the all visible light from heaven, and in *Woodwose* and *The Lost Shadow of Things* there is also beauty, heroism, greatness, determined by a ray of eternal values, but also reinforces themes of needs, desire, intoxication, defiance, grief, worry, poverty, doubt, bewilderment at a fallen worlds and horror.

God shows himself in human activity and being. You are in Him, everything yourself, where the special purpose of love is felt, and shown in how simple and deep is the knowledge that comes from the heart.

Only the present world conditions could create this poetry, and it is in that and His unbounded Grace that gave its genesis and completion; to be shared. The sensual renewal of spiritual change that opens the mind and melts hardness of heart, dissolving traditional attachments and obligations, awakening a message of spiritual re-birth of matter and spirit, and of a new centre that of necessity creates a new freedom.

The opposition between control and self-will, the commandment of the spirit that only nature and spirit can restore the original man. The renewed in spirit are no longer lured by false light or narcotic poisons, or the withering magic of the dying age.

Those who are reborn to the God in them, the Holy Spirit, The Lord within them, grasp the whole. He has fresh ground and an open path and no longer has to wander or lurk,- he just has to listen to God and observe His commands. He does not need multiple new stimuli to numb and distract himself over his old needs and emptiness. He just needs prayer and supplication! There is a new sense in his waking heart that gives birth to new joys, responsibilities and poetry!

It is a heart inflamed with love that is both strengthening of, and in active service to the whole. It is not a hollow imagination or loose thinking without action or arid knowledge without work. God is already visible in the smallest sphere. Only when people and God live together again can the holy song of praise rises again and the people sing the song of God that their prophets have long declared.

Only when people co-operate and create with God, not as egos stuck in their narrow spheres, but beings whose true centre is God; this alone promises a new possibility for humanity. The homecoming is the return of God from Heaven to Earth. Man has emptied himself, advanced and has lost his way.

Poetry helps one to find one's way again, inside oneself, in its simple origins; the godlike being at the other-side of the doorway in each man's heart.

Harry Matthews, Shropshire, Dec. 2020.

{ 2 }

The Hollow of the Old Packing-case

Although he drank, ate little, the dining-
Room was empty when the folk who cluster
In the churchyard appeared, with spectres who
Cluster in the churchyard!

Even the fertile vale has evil shades,
Like black thunder imploding in his throat,
Said the boy.
Yes, in his throat,
Said the Spectre.

But see the church in the hollow,
And hollow correspondence, the fence between,
Yes, hollow correspondence, the fence between.

HARRY MATTHEWS

Maltravers did not listen to vanities,
And looked ahead into the empty years.
Yes, ahead into the empty years.

Her world was in pieces, entertainments are closed.
Yes, in pieces entertainments are closed.

As empty as an English choir stall, cried
The bitch.

(Devils sleep on the couch at the foot of her bed,
To sympathize with her disposition.
Yes, to sympathize with her condition.)

Besides, the empty jar will save trouble and
Rooms were empty.
I've been empty too often myself.
I live in a dry cellar, empty save for the grotto.

The roads are empty, the fields are deserted,
The houses of the hollow in which it
Lay had ceased to have existence.

Bein' born on Hollow eve, says he,
(*Aye, Eve Vigil of All Hallows*, I replied)

I couldn't be nothin' else.
I couldn't be nothin' else.

True to the God in You

It and hollow consolations.

His cheeks were hollow
And hectic, his eyes were,
And hectic, were his eyes.

{ 3 }

True to the God in You

Like a seed from the craw of a wild swan
Shot, transgressors don't put themselves higher.
Put yourself lower? I said: *Shepherd, what*
Wound is in you that makes you suffer?
Yield?

To live without reproach, *sans* accolade,
Retreat from the world, you're despised by it.
If you should gain His grace you must never
Be so foolish as to risk losing it.

You hide what is murky in your life
So that they will admire you more,
But there is no glory in these bad multitudes,
It only makes them more jealous, being
Rebellious angels, disloyal to God.

True to the God in You

The sky chases you; you are out of Hope,
But to be completely different. So, find yourself,
Be then in the Lord, unto your true Self.
There is no real glory in a bad flock
- And nothing but Him is ever more yourself.

{ 4 }

Agony

Screams of anger– full, muffled voices
That any cowardice could stir.
Cowardice could stir?

We are at the place of people
The witch has committed a crime
...A crime
...What comfort she received.
What comfort?

And let me into the secret things.
The secret things?
Hear in their circle,
For people that seem pierced by pain
...*Pierced by pain?*
And this hand-drowned:

True to the God in You

They made a noise as if rolling
In eternity– that was full of dubious throbbing:
Shepherding this thick air, uninterrupted,
The frogs leap in the storm.
In the storm?
Yes, they are galvanised...

I spoke...resounding in the starless air
Sighs, sobs, and a loud cry to me:

Such pathetic musings must experience
The rod of conduction, the wretched soul
Of which I spoke to you is lightening,
Where I strike you to the last groan,
When you started crying,
I was crying.

Strange languages, terrible sounds,
Words of on top of it, as knowledgeable
Of what is due. He puts his hand around
Me as a noose, with a cheerful look...
Here it is fitting, that every doubt is
Broken. But it is knotted,
Is it not?

{ 5 }

When There Was No Eternity

There was no created Eternity, no
Created forever. I left every hope
That you walk through me. You
See the thing in front of me Eternally
Tremendous responsibility comes,
A platform of purpose where you can stand.
- Just as I stood strong, out of the lost cell.

I climb the ladder of my destiny...
Some go to hell to suffer forever,
Others go to Heaven to be free...

Through me you went to the city of death,
And in mourning, through me you climbed upwards,
Through me alone to Life. Through me alone.

{ 6 }

God's Love Shines Brighter

The Creator rightly gave me my place.
The power divine has increased me greatly,
The first love, the highest brightness of Love,
The highest brightness, Fire from Mount Zion.

I receive the key from the throne of grace,
I receive the key and open the door...
I open the padlock of darkness...

Before, there was no Eternity. No
Created Forever. My flesh wasted...
When every load of the wicked weighed hard,
And congregations of darkness decreed
That I would not be going anywhere...

HARRY MATTHEWS

Then the blood stirred, and fire fall...
Every mark of darkness wiped away,
Every fire quenching habit fast expired.
When satanic sleeping tablets dissolved,
I awoke in new dimensions of God.

{ 7 }

When We Changed Our Flocks At Night

We did have awhile to take our leave there
At the bottom end, I heard a loud one
Slow expire from blast; flashlight in a sphere.

Then came the mushroom, red flumes of dark smoke,
We were near by, so not far from the epicentre,
That I overlooked the curious shape in the clouds...

What a disagreeable genootschnap,[1]
Interposed the younger one of the jumble.
"Well, go on,", another exclaimed speaking
Into the shadows where formed the circle
Of silent men gathered around a lamb.
As soon as the lamb saw me he vanished
With a cry beyond the men to the hill...

HARRY MATTHEWS

You dislike artists & poets of all sorts,
You would rather praise poseurs & counterfeits in their place,
Who are they who hanker after recognition?

He looked on them with a smile of recognition,
My panderers, what sort of shyness is this?
I turned back from them, revealing myself to myself,
As one big person, as someone who has arrived,

But in the dream, heaven showed me my real picture,
My real self, & it wasn't so big, & that was the beginning
Of the true recognition...would that not be a real policy?
Not what men are calling you to be, but as God sees,

With a cold frigid stare, I pondered the dream, & could see
It was about myself. A woman was gliding towards me...
We want you to join your foolish sophistries to lead
People the wrong way.

… { 8 }

Nova Testamentum

You became ridiculous
The snake gods came instead of You.
Pythons choke out your breath,
You had almost fallen.

Spread brazenly at crack mouth:
The snake is ours: we come to cut his head.
It still goes downward– yet it lifts.
It still has a fork– for its tongue!

Soft spoken chap, full of malice,
Subservient to the dust.
The sword of vengeance will take him.

He's still limps– artless, coarse; a dick.
He's still reluctant– what a hick!
No leg: we only need a crowd of butterflies.

HARRY MATTHEWS

No grip: we need no peevish bullies.

Out there with souls with lows and hells,
A worm glorified with a boon,
We need only angels to run and quell
To conquer evil witchcraft spells.

{ 9 }

Ambiguous Loss

After the dream told me the names
Of those ancient curs, who hid me
With hate that almost felt welcome,

I ended a poet! That I
May go against them fully.

There they talk as a double head,
But are separate in their conspiracy of evil,
How they overlapped, the bastards!

And they seemed to flow so easily
As faithful friends; sincerity
Feigned. It was all a mask they used.

And she: wait until God pursues her,
And whether the hate switches you

HARRY MATTHEWS

With a git to please her and him;

You see in dreams her evil switch.
You see how they turn in vice-ditch,
The water of belief makes you rich.

{ 10 }

Heavy Fell The Wrath

Fire of the Spirit engulfs me,
I decree your soul is in trouble,

Leave now or feel the wrath of God.

Deaf, the evil ears in the walls,
In with the demand, air thickens,

The light stillness, *sans* evil load,
A bitter end your cure carries...

You flee from their evil circles,
The dildo from the pit of hell,

Fanatic knocking at the door,
The loose tongue swings over water...

HARRY MATTHEWS

In the wind the match extinguished.
Then came light through the tempest.

What a bouquet of inducement,
Arranged in colour and odour,
From a poisoned inclination.

O varmint cruel and darkening.
How you scythe through the fruitful swath.

Your fear contaminates the world:
Satan looks at us with indecency,

Never beg him for you to win
For he comforts you with cruel lies.

{ 11 }

Elegy for a Degenerate

How can I hear your honest thought?
I'll get inside and turn it round,
And surely the torment will come…

It is the height that gives rebirth
On the ridge toward Parnassus,
That I and my muse are hastened.

The poetry in my heart groans,
Drew me from the beautiful one
Who tore from me my sin and grief.

May my Love remain Holy Love,
Love frees, is not an oppression,
Is it love that drew you apart?

Love rends us asunder, to live

HARRY MATTHEWS

As one who's saved going to Cain.
This was the disdain he offered us.

I heard of his wild sordid reign,
I heard he was insatiable,
He inclined himself to the dirt.

Don't ask a pervert what this meant!
His trembling fingers speak of guilt.
Torn and flung into deeper hurt.

Then my truth breathed out to save me:
How many sweets are served by queens,
On doilies laced with painful fate?

The Glade Beyond the Forest

I

Then I turn to the boy more precisely,
And I started: *Shepherd, your wound's
Full of Joy to the point of ecstasy.*

The Shepherd replied:
*Then tell me: at the bitter day
Why are they jealous of the flock,
You envy the shepherd's duty?*

I said: *Pleasure is sweet,
But the grace of God is sweeter.
I am in the Master's comfort.*

HARRY MATTHEWS

The Shepherd frowned,
Willful ignorance is your lot,
In accordance with your hate, your style,
To play the judge with such pretence.

I replied: *We live to labour everyday.*

II

How the Shepherd loved him.
The lad saw no untruth in him.

(You are so entranced by his bright eyes,
Read the sparks of his memories.
His chiselled features captivate:

There he sits in slothful despond,
Satan's friends, wrested from the light–
Hearts of gall and tongues of wormwood.

Smacked me on the face terribly.
Then offended me with insult.
That day my love was given up.

The angel message made you grasp,
The others hard-hearted, scoffing,
You gain your senses, brighter now,
And you rise up like the sun).

An Angel Spoke on the Cool Breeze

The scandalous mention resounds
Above the young man in your life,
Can you join your friendship to God?

I haven't got a poet friend,
I never had a poet friend.
I don't have any friends as poets.
Could you be my first poet friend?
Said the boy ambiguously.

Honoured unequivocally
Sincere in the affirmative,
Just leave me to get back to you,
I'm sure you'll do the same for me
Unless I hope ambitiously.

In which case you will punish me.

The boy paused, and then came closer...

You must lend me your poet eyes,
So I may see with your rose tint lens.
I'll have to think it over dear,
A glint of humour in his eyes,
The poet wished it were mischief,
A gleam at least to lighten up,
The grave kindliness of his glance,
A trace of blue lit in his eyes,
Then anger came, and he looked stern
Though I wished his gander was more aft.
He treated me as if most daft.

The poet thought to write more words:
The pen, his sword in his left hand.
The lines that came were first inspired:

It was Barnfield[2] the poet, sees
His influence was well chosen,
Virgil who wrote the Bucolics,
Theocritus the pastoral,
Sidney & Spenser,
And now this poet-taster...

I sound a different note then they,

True to the God in You

Discern, different styles like many
Mouths but are one and of the same.
Humiliating me, they do
Their manufactured flavourings
Plundered from archetypal
Trammels...

Where verse is but the looking glass,
Ars Poetica[3], the mirror
To the pre-existing ideal?

I saw the beautiful boy here,
In league with the exalted song
That floats on the air, across the
Full width of the whole circling.

He sang a little longer there
Whereupon I shed a tear drop,
My boy smiled then left, demurely...

{ 14 }

Some untimely thought did instigate

But a few did, in that place reproach of me,
By giving me their wicked eyes, their turn will come:

The lord will punish those who do evil,
Those that gather against me are unmasked,

You will hear in the drum beat their downfall,
You shall not succumb to the evil one's,
Who work evil in the shadows.

How they betray their own faces with shame,
With God I will fulfil my destiny,
With His great spirit I complete my goal.

{ 15 }

The Angel of Comfort

Leaving the bondage of stagnancy
The heart of Christ conquers everything.

He saw more than the body-mind.
His poetic sagacity,
His jesting and his moral sense.
His feelings were his faculties,
Somewhere at the back of his brain?

Living in his cerebellum
So the phrenologists would say,
Lived his faculty of colour,
Resulting from the harmony
Between the colours in his mind.

His sight was keen vivacious,
Carried far up to the lighthouse

HARRY MATTHEWS

From where he purveyed the rainbow.
Smoothing the asperities of
Adversity, in the lightning fall.

At a new place expectedly
The angels bathed in glorious light,
White stargazer, and rose-pink tinge...
They were dressed in luminous blue,
Violet robe, swathed with golden hair,
Transcending their Holy precinct.

His grace form, and his lovely face,
The angel of comfort, weeping:
Look– he said– Be still I am there
My peace often envelopes you.
His face aflame, of highest rank,
Being utterly consumed with
The great light fire Love of the Lord.

{ 16 }

Lyric Harmonic on the String of Sensuality

The Shepherd looked on in despair
Right there when the witch said her curse.
Distant Alexis fell silent.

He turned to me more trustingly,
Enjoying my lyric poesy,
He opened the way with his own.

If you have sanity, listen,
Pay attention to instruction,
Under the verse-scribbling shepherd.

He sang in a calming love tone,
With a melodious accent,
The summer grass swayed by sheepfold.

HARRY MATTHEWS

The sounds brought a foresight of rest.
The Disputation is railing,
Disturbed unruly powers attack.
Walk unrestingly through the storm.

The cracked branches break, soon they fall.
You fling off the caressing hand.
(You began life at the treetop,

Now you are flung to the gutter),
Roused to revolt, you run raging.
You drive the shepherd; his flock flees.

He closed my eyes: then raised his head
To the hill that's always seen there
At the place where light shines brightest…

As with the wolf that lurks for them
Sheep scatter from the babbling brook,
As though each one of them were drunk.

I saw a dozen sheep flee from
One of the river passes,
Bleating toward dry sheltering.

He wiped the sheep filth from his face;
The horror and degradation.
For such exertions he was paid.

True to the God in You

I knew that God would guide him on.
I looked to the Lord, he answered,
In silence I released my hold.

Audacious gesture, he looked up!
He came to the gate they opened.
Did he close it? There was glad consent.

{ 17 }

The Painful Frustrations of the Poet

The Marsh Shade, the hostile, fake
Respectful witch...You learn what pain
Is needed for your art, poet.

Following his own opinion
Rather than the received wisdom,
The grief of exile threatening.

She held you in scorn. Together,
Giving suffering to each other,
More pain than comfort could teach.

{ 18 }

Power Divine Taught You to Tend

Through the flaming dawn of Norbury,[4]
You walk lively from the manor,
Please stay here with me for awhile,

Since I teach myself in your tongue,
You are from that homely pasture,
Of that, I may complain too much.

A gunshot echoes on the ridge,
The prophet stone is in the wood,
I sit on it; a peaceful guide.

You said to me I must return,
The shepherd has his prophet crook,
The acorn is the seed of strength.

HARRY MATTHEWS

The shepherd tends so steadfastly,
His flock he raised from meekest lambs,
As though he was in love with God.

Hands bold and ready to perform
Urged me to his peaceful refuge,
Why does your love weigh on his heart?

And when I stood above his flock,
He pierced me with his long hard look,
I told him of the ancestors.

Willing to serve God and obey,
I described everything to him
It was then you started to cry.

And said: grim enemies are they,
For me, for my flock and this land,
That's why I drove the witch out twice.

He drove the wolves away, dispersed
Every sheep, and in the dipping,
Their fleeces sparkled in the sun.

The field edge had uncovered earth,
The worn path of many sheep hooves,
Where shadow fell on the bright grass.

True to the God in You

He looked around preoccupied,
To see where the absent sheep was,
And then he heard a distant bleat...

The shepherd went towards the sheep
Up to the brow of the hillock.

Where is my boy? Why has he left?

His own strength had returned him safe
The shepherd took him in his arms,
The sheep recognised him gladly.

What immeasurable favour came,
God heard his prayer, and gave blessings,
God always answers, perfectly...

He jumped and shouted 'come back' sheep,
Do not yet leave the safety here
Of flock. *The sun shall lick your face!*

And when I put it off awhile
His answer, he would not reply,
He fell and wouldn't come back up.

{ 19 }

He Found the Place

Such a warm-eyed youth came to me,
And knew I was who he wanted-
Grace and a miracle conspired.

And when he pulled my hands to his,
I clasped him gladly.
His eyes twinkled. He surrendered.

With his *geisha* smile beaming wide,
I recognised our past life joys...
Fancy meeting you in this place!

And he replied: *My shepherd dear,*
I longed to take these steps with you
And again, go forward in our love.

With all my strength I will please you.

True to the God in You

Come, let us lose the trace of time,
In your eyes I see great pleasure.

He places you in his fond heart,
Walking ponderously in truth,
Loneliness lighted by triumph.

Just come and let him guide you on!
Afterwards you go to your flock
Where you laugh for the eternal.

I dare to be on his level,
And run with raised head on the field,
Like the Greek warrior of old.

{ 20 }

The Place to Teach (Bite Before Bit?)

Mercy floats above the tree-tops.
Let it sink before the rose-dawn,
And who will guide you on this path?

Get over your miserable life.
I found myself inside that field
The fullness youth has given me.

I left it late today– first time
I got there when he fast approached.
Now he follows me on the path.

He said: *You seek the shepherd's star?*
Don't you miss the glorious man.
You will love his beautiful life.

True to the God in You

I fell asleep in early morn,
Troubled by the horn blown warning,
The red sky in the morning cries.

But that grateful, goodly young man,
The one who ascended from here,
He looks down from the holy hill.

Will be hostile to you for your good
And rightly so, between sweet thighs
It is nice to rub tender meats.

Far away from the hostile town,
And the arrogant plebs of envy,
Keep yourself removed from evil.

Your misery knows much disgrace,
That this accusation ails you,
Recoil from the bait and bite!

{ 21 }

He Taught You How to Find

Some of the sheep had died that night,
The wolf ate those that strayed afar.

The holy lamb came here to life
From the Cross where Christ was murdered;
Took on himself all our evil...

My refusal would be granted,
I petitioned I should remain,
Watch the boy that is my request.

To my mind, he could not flatter,
Still his paternal shepherd face
When he declared his heart that day!

True to the God in You

How can he be so eccentric?
How far I held his affection:
Away! That it would disappear!

{ 22 }

Banished From Our Tree of Life

I remember it well because
It became the turning point of
My destiny; my star rising...

Beneath the waterfall we stood,
Filled with mutual admiration.
Your eyes and mine locked in a trance.

I feel you felt what I had felt,
It was not only I who felt...
The truth is you felt love for me.

This was no dream, but our fountain,
The living water of the Lord,
That poured down upon us; flowing.

True to the God in You

Our hearts lived in a paradise.
The garden was glowing with peace.
For two souls who reflected love.

We sat beneath the ancient tree,
Faint whispering, forget-me-nots,
How did the deadly nightshade grow?

But deadly was the smile she wore,
When she invaded our love sweet grove,
And her jealousy drove us loose.

{ 23 }

No One Shall Harm You

They robbed you of your Opinion
You did not acknowledge the crime.
You have robbed yourself. Yes, yourself.

What are you doing in the wood?
Night-fall, and flames are rising.
The thieves are full of writhing snakes.

We should shepherd the sheep. The Sheep?
Why not strain for a second time?
Why not kill me beside this hedge.

Dig around the stump all you like.
The roots have grown deep with the years.
A hedge grows quickly. Cut the hedge.

Here, take your sheers and do your work

True to the God in You

You found stronger hands...fire crackles
At lower drop, the wood pile burns.

–And there's no trace of pity there
You shuddered by the smoke and fumes
And part it with the hands you raise.

You?

Emerging from the smouldering,
Screaming from blood, the bark and crack,
You drop your human sack and stand.

So this is what you've now become.
That from these chars you put your hand
So your dropped words I might have cracked,

I flutter like a bird unharmed,
While there's a man in Ithaca[5]
No one shall rob or do you harm.

{ 24 }

A Heart in Darkness

There was a quiet, slim complaint,
The odds stacked on the other side
But I saw him, knew to read
Subdued applause, half-spoken prayers,

Hush of wrongdoing, a dodgy
Consultation, dirty card deck,
Soft nothings, jottings in murmurs–

Excuse me now, thrice double ass?

He could not bear to see her flirt.
A white stain smeared on a trouser.
Will it bring him exculpation?
What a bold ejaculation.

What a flirt, but he's not allowed

True to the God in You

Favourites, only dark flutters,
The old pretence that nods gravely,
And the secret of his discharge.

It would be as fruitless, dangerous,
If surmised he'd FINALLY reach
Forgiveness. Until then, that is why
I swat flies here, completely mad.

*

You are fallen, scandalise them,
Into such an outrage of
Offensive local opinion,
You feel death would be preferable,

So heavy your guilt, you blame me,
But in the very circumstance,
There was a way out of the shame,
In time God's mercy excused him.

Why I sit here, completely sane.

The Northern-most Pilgrim

{ 25 }

In the bright broken-path, I walked,
From the still simplicity of cloister and ladder–
I look outward from the tangle,
Brushwood, that nest of greenery,
A heavy grove of pines, weather–
Beaten trees and shrubs all about,
Lying everywhere, expected,
I can't get out, nor quite endure,
Like a stranger looking with awe,
Trying to get at the mystery...

Listening to the wind-whistle,
Exploiting the rich gift of time,
No time to waste on division,
Trails of the heart in the byways,

True to the God in You

Thoughts that twist the mind in spirals,
Forward swings, the head goes bobbing,
Spiral of the wood edge ending,
Pulling through the cranky dark vale,
Past the ledge of the blended hedges:
Raising your gaze into the Light.

How murky the light. What throbbing,
As though trolls track the veil of space,
Pursued by a whirlwind, dark clouds,
Misjudgment tasted in the gloom,
Waters rush in stream of twilight,
The dying sun sprays bright ember...

Now all the shadows have crimson
Through waves of daunting heavy trees.
Naked star above the treetop
Light that travels back to dazzle.

The red house opens on the glade,
Destination of the pilgrim.

{ 26 }

Let Who Listens Close That door

She watches us, gnawed with envy,
The strange falling of your starlight,
You heave with a sigh of despair.

You have already become harsh,
Obstreperous and troublesome,
Like a vulgar, angry urchin...

Dare we ask at all why you come?
We prowl the night edge of your pain.
You, a vicious and surly steward,

A purser splicing the main brace.
The sad frowns of the second-mates,
The evening, a sad memory;

True to the God in You

It is sworn to your secrecy:
You feel like you've been to a tryst,
What you forsook you bade *adieu*,

Your hand trembles, dew-dripped longing.
Then a new dream possesses you,
Where your briskness belies depth,

To your false striving temptation,
As if your lust was still with me,
Unequally matched like my love.

{ 27 }

Wampish Refrain of Your Whining Obstruction

You had no *beau* from Flowery Land:
Cicisbeov[6], cockalorum[7],
Colloguing[8] contumely[9], like a
Coxcomb[10], fool in that outlaw's cap.

You had bright eyes, down rabbit-hole,
A prayer to cancel all your fears.
In your restless, foreboding tears,
A new pole drew your compass soul.

Your shallow breath through all the stress,
No bed of ease, that vexing cease,
Decreasing as you inhale peace,

True to the God in You

Swimming as to over-impress...

And God, unbidden, rose in you.
Ended the sad hullabaloo.[11]

{ 28 }

The Quockerwodger

Slow remembered, muzzled with praise:
Virtue lost on lips of beauty,

How crapulous[12] your murmuring,
Esurient[13], Dandiprat[14] with
His drab doxy...[15]

Let by another Jade[16], it stirs,
That is because the gudgeon[17] errs,
Now purring like a Grimalkin,[18]

Yes, your gorgonizing goody,
Because the gudgeon has been let
By another Jade: the fizgig[19]
Fishwife, who you excogigate
With to furbish your gadzooks[20], as
A gardyloo[21], whose milder heart

True to the God in You

Hears the call and is thus chosen.

Your Lethophobia[22] makes you
Malapert, mazed by moil[23], how
Monsterful are your needs, as you
Peregrinate. Who kissed you with spirit-fire,
That pernicious periapt[24] you
Carry on a cushion, conjured
By the Pythoness; Quaggy witch.
That makes you a Quockerwodger![25]

{ 29 }

Escape From The Sluberdegullion Snake

You seethe quothas[26], rathe ripe rapscallion[27,]
Reaving the place like a rapacious rover,
Rainbow covered. What sanative for a
Scapegrace?[28] Her scolds are like a season in
The shambles, in your shrive you seek for shrift,[29]
But her sluberdegullion[30] snake, is quick
To smite, strait with the stripe; can't suffer a strumpet,[31]

And the twattle of the twitter light
Tricked by the turnkey, so the varlet wins,[32]
For another twelve month, maybe more,
Whereagainst, the wonder-wench swims leaving
You wood mad, with no zounds or yoicks,
So don't complain, for you were chosen,

True to the God in You

Your days are charmed;
A floating world…
Esteem the years
That birthed your inner man,
Redeemed, the time,
God lives in you.

{ 30 }

The Waterfall Where We Once Stood

Waterfall, where I stood with you,
Looking at the seascape in the
Morning, is now so glorious,
Reflecting from the sun a light
Like the slow trickle of honey...

Water running from a great height
You stand like a Moomin[33] looking,
Then down plunge into the drop.
At the sweeping freshness of Grace,
Sun, your bright cosmic day...
But it was too early for us.

Daybreak, illumination gleam,
Clarity-raising water spray;

True to the God in You

Rising where the fall hits the stream.
You take all the joy with you now.

{ 31 }

The Perverted Belfry

The tower still rises from red earth
On rugged worship's foundation.
The bells ring the blessing on us.
Ignorance is ease: the done thing.

My strong prayer now counterblasts,
Knowing that it conquers the disease.

For Satan's bells they ring away,
Through black robe of the hierophant,[34]
The gable end is burning flame.

But painfully avoid their ploy,
God condemns the violation,
And God will hang them from the ropes,
Expelling those who barred themselves
From his Kingdom of rest and peace.

True to the God in You

God's wrath bolt shall strike, break the bell,
Repeal the dark consecration…
When he shall break the seventh seal,
Step into grace at the altar.

The priest who curses the true man,
As she gives out crumbs for the birds,
And the spit she spat in the cup,
Makes her choke on God's Holy Word.

(And the warden has lost his key,
And the priest drowns in the red sea.)

{ 32 }

The Ecclesiastical Survey

You call us, we cry for safety,
Off with your health and safety goals.
The candles were lit with sadness
Votive hopes are quickly blown out,
The officious breath prevailed.
Does the Church of the stupid die?

What you do on the first day?
You gather in Church to the Sun?
In paper envelopes you seal
Your investment in the charade.
The Resurrection offering,
The guilt money Our Saviour paid?

From all the ugliness you fear,

True to the God in You

You can find it flashing in here,
And losing the body's longing
Your smile sits on a nest of snakes.

You were glowing for us in dust,
Voice in the burning shrubbery.
You gave the unstilted[35] lilies
Like you have always refreshed me.

With your old form to scatter us
They sing too loudly to be heard.
From ignorance of the shadow
The prim pews do nothing but moan
Proclaiming a hurtful restraint,
Damns you and maintains themselves.

You call it wholesome? Like eating?
Tame heretics who shatters us–
Unzip the sheep's fleece, play-actors,
This religion of pharisee.
Give me the fire, Holy Spirit,
And burn so many demons there
That we won't ever see our sins.

… { 33 }

What Carried The Day

Release Your word upon my Life,
From the Throne of Grace, ask for rest,
Unchanged, how the changer redeems,
And referring us to you, you
Escaped the noise of the swarming.
Judgment falls upon the wicked.
You are consecrated for the
Rest of the seventh day reborn.
We enjoyed our day, one distant,
Only this sign remained, beloved,
How the world sought to annoy you.
Your star lit destiny is writ:
How the higher light pierced your heart,
The mighty beam of heaven's eye
In the whisper of sad silence.
Summer peace, like there never was,
I see you are flourishing now,

True to the God in You

In this season of prophecy,
The Lion's roar; , Heaven's thunder!

Spin It Clean Off The Reel

All night I had in that heartache
A fast pull of the harpoon rope,
That unreal dream of the whaler
Raised its sails just for hunting,
And out flow, escape from the port.

The hero sailed without blemish,
More joyful than when a shepherd:
Wealthy, worldly commendations,
Singing before the lonely sea.

Who made the turquoise flow in me
That I a snotty might be soaked.
Free me with that rigid deck gun,
See I revere the occulting;

True to the God in You

Pilot offing to prick a chart...

Finally, you haul taught, then heave,
Hear me beg to the deep blue sea,
On the blacklist, the bitter end
You blow the gaff on the blower

Between wind and water the bilge,
Where blood is thicker than water.
Get your finger out, brace of shakes,
There's room enough to swing a cat!

You old hand, a nosey parker,
Running the gauntlet round the bend.
Its touch and go, don't swing the lead!
Spinning a yarn, springing a leak,

I belong to you: so take heart,
This ship, a heart of oak that burns,
Enters into eternal flame.

{ 35 }

(Un)Cloaked in Mystery

A young man, wearing nothing but a linen garment,
was following Jesus. When they seized him,
he fled naked, leaving his garment behind.
Mark 14:51-52

When the follower was fleeing,
What ignominious flight; failure,
He left his shirt, abandonment,
They fell from faith and chose such shame,
They have fallen in their courage.

Angelic, young man dressed in white,
Jesus gives garment of Glory,
To those that fail God offers hope,
Buried with the garment of shame,
Resurrected, glory clothing,
From naked shame he is restored.

True to the God in You

There is Light beyond the dark cave,
You penetrate the root of art,
At one step of your eagle eye.
You penetrate the mystery there,
And purify your heart and mind.
The bright brim of Eternity.
My star now emerges through You.

(Mighty Redeemer has mercy,
Have mercy on worry's sin).

One By One Hill won

You met the messenger of Joy,
Through a full Spring game of roulette,
A floating island on the lake,
The flower buds opened and oozed.

Hidden love in that obscure place.
Did you find the wonderful one?
And your love became the angel,
Adores you from the mountain shade.

Your tale points to a dry desert,
Your thirst a mirage sacrifice,
From our instant sighted love well,
In my heart a shard of grit grates...

Then Lightning bolt blasted downward,
At the bowl edge of star lit sky,

True to the God in You

It burst, an inflamed momentum:

The spit down fire was split in two,
Merging at the root of the tree,
Waiting for destruction, fire wild.
Those that are free burn the waters,
No snake or spirit wanders there,
They cannot strive once they are killed.

I saw him fly from the mountain.
What my urge asked of him in vain:
Far country– you were determined
Since you met me out of the mist.

Our lonely summits formed a bridge,
You look but cannot walk its ropes,
For fear of shame, in case you fall.
What was perverted in your thoughts
God heals for He has sent His Light.

… 37 …

Bionicle of Falling into Deeper Darkness

The black moon rises high above,
Closure through your reef
Blood oozes through your deep thigh gash
Your big field is wide
Smooth as if cut with a razor
You live with a hag in your house.

The beast in your cage palpitates,
Pain rushes to your throbbing head:
Wicked incision from the witch,
Pierced for the ungoldly implant.
The laceration is stitched up.

Now fill the trove with grave offence!
The sun sets but the flag remains,

True to the God in You

Augmenting their inclinations,
Serious about the mountains,
Trivialising the night-fall,
In the valley of *faux* violence,
Trying to create the future,
A desert of foolish upgrades,
Never satiated by it,
Experiments by troglodytes!

What violence this biohacking,
Where misanthropists force
Intranasal oxytocin,
No fun to circumvent the fear,
By the way of oblivion,
Breaks the ethics of an epoch
Sprinkling ballistic gellatin
Like wild felines souring the day,
Torturing after their hunger.

Withered flowers strewn in the garden:
Let it be unconventional!
Some things are not permissible...
If he is to be biohacked
In such twilight of Satan-hood,
Perhaps he penetrated soon
Our moon? Godly inheritance...

Over the mangled miracle,

HARRY MATTHEWS

You share your Holy agenda-
He is One, not because your toil
Not because your instinct is Death,
But that life fires mistruth quickly
So let the sun eclipse the moon,
And at the war's end be kicked in!

{ 38 }

Flowing waves to Rapture

I feel water from that planet as
My pale face sees through the veil.
He just turned to me a dolphin.
Will he return to me a blue whale?

And ocean, the way I knew love,
I am starting to write you now,
And you are vast, immeasurable,
Your absence made presence somehow,

Yes, the caller of Fantasy…

You can never be extinguished,
Eternal spiral in deep flame,
The ocean tumult rages on,

HARRY MATTHEWS

To that unexpected sea-game.

Yes, the summons of your rebirth.

I dissolve in echoes, weaving
Circles, bubbles of unnamed praise:
I don't surrender to shark's teeth,
I claim victory in those seaways.

Yes, courage of a warrior.

A sudden wave crashed over me
Upon the surface where we catch
A short breath before descending...
The foe we fight we must outmatch.

Yes, this conflict is quite daunting.

Fervent clicks, the language you know,
Holograms and soundscapes merging
In ocean where you're flipping,
The message illuminating...

Yes, now you see the unseen.
Then I see how longing melts me,
The moon from which silver light glows,
It opens the nearest distance,
And warms the loosening ice flows...

True to the God in You

Yes, you are closer than before.

Past the great white and beluga,
I swim with the mauling dolphins,
Where Orca's gorge tremendous sharks,
Where whales float like huge submarines...

Yes, I feel I'm writing that scene...
Swim the sea of crystal waters,
To the planet that is ailing,
Spark of the *Spiralactica*,
I"m just the human voice yearning.

On the Pleasure of Sunbathing

What a blessing to sun bask,
At last, past the rainy threshold.
The warm rays lick me all over,
How soothing this bright midday bath.

My sun-drenched hair, the tender light,
The sweat forming from every pore,
My body is slow cooked bronzing,
My cheeks kissed by the blazing rays...

The afternoon that burns with heat,
Apollo rising to the sun,
A minor breeze plays upon me,
And an iced tea quenches my thirst...

True to the God in You

Then I think of the long winter
How I'm lit by the inner fire
From the sauna to the ice bath,
In depth an invisible light.

Then with sun filled joy I slumber,
Through that long-awaited dream time!
As though embalmed with after sun.
The scent of myrrh, I start to purr,
Like a satisfied dreamy cat.

{ 40 }

On Conversing with Blackbirds

In my dream
I was at the top of the hill,
Below me was grey wasteland,
From tarmac sprung luminous grass.
In the hedgerow the black birds spoke:
We are looking for raspberries
What are you looking for my dear?

Unruffled, yet I could not answer.
The reality of their speech
Did not encourage my reply...

There is a white Lilly I seek,
But all I can find are violets,
And they, quite a few, are shrinking...

Haros the Hedgehog

A full restored Hedgehog, Haros
Where early the tempting hedgerows,
It would at last appear, we hedgehogs
Were made for hedges and our
Inevitable Love of hedges compareth
Not to the joys of ye old Hedgehoggery
Hedgehog hotel,
The latter, the just destination and joy
Of any true born Hedgehog, wishing
To renounce the hibernational joys
Of the Hedge!

{ 42 }

Footnotes

1. A **genootschap** is a specifically Dutch form of company, association, society or cooperative, named after the pursuit for which its members gather.
2. **Richard Barnfield** (baptized 29 June 1574 – 1620) was an English poet.

    Barnfield was born at the home of his maternal grandparents in Norbury, Staffordshire, where he was baptized on 29 June 1574. He was the son of Richard Barnfield, gentleman, and Mary Skrymsher (1552–1581). He was brought up in Shropshire at the Manor House in Edgmond, his upbringing upbringing supervised by his aunt Elizabeth Skrymsher after his mother died when Barnfield was six years. See: Dickens, Gordon (1987). *An Illustrated Literary Guide to Shropshire*. Shropshire Libraries. p. 3.

3. ***Ars Poetica***, or "The Art of Poetry", is a poem written by Horace c. 19 BC, in which he advises poets on the art of writing poetry. The Ars Poetica exercised a great influence on European literature and has inspired poets and authors since it was written. The *Ars Poetica* was first translated into English in 1566 by Thomas Drant. A translation by Ben Jonson was published posthumously in 1640.
4. **Norbury** is a village and civil parish in the Borough of Stafford, in west Staffordshire, England.
5. **Ithaca**, Ιθάκη, *Ithaki*, a Greek island located in the Ionian Sea, off the northeast coast of Kefalonia and to the west of continental Greece. Modern Ithaca is generally identified with Homer's Ithaca, the home of Odysseus, whose delayed return to the island is the plot of the classical Greek tale the *Odyssey*.

    In the Odyssey of Homer, Ithaca is described thus
    ...dwell in clear-seen Ithaca, wherein is a mountain, Neriton, covered with waving forests, conspicuous from afar; and round it lie many isles hard by one another, Dulichium, and Same, and wooded Zacynthus. Ithaca itself lies close in to the mainland the furthest toward the gloom, but the others lie apart toward the Dawn and the sun—a rugged isle, but a good nurse of young men. Homer 9.21–27. *The Odyssey with an English Translation* (in Ancient Greek and English). Translated by Murray, Augustus Taber. London, 1919.

Letitia Elizabeth Landon accepts Ithaca as the home of Ulysses in her poem *Town and Harbour of Ithaca*, 'The glorious island where Ulysses was the king'. In 1911, Cavafy wrote "Ithaca", inspired by the Homeric return journey of Odysseus to his home island, as depicted in the Odyssey. The poem's theme is the destination which produces the journey of life: "Keep Ithaka always in your mind. / Arriving there is what you're destined for".

6. **Cicisbeo**, in 18th- and 19th-century Italy, the cicisbeo or cavalier servente was the man who was the professed gallant or lover of a woman married to someone else.

7. **Cockalorum,** Possibly English *cock* ("rooster"), with *-a-* and Latin *-lorum* suffixed as a fanciful elaboration; or from a Dutch onomatopoeic dialect term *kockeloeren* ("the cry of a rooster; cock-a-doodle-doo"), hence the modern Dutch verb *koekeloeren* ("to crow").

8. **Collogue**, First attested in 1590s (as *colloguing*), presumably from *colleague* ("to associate") and French *colloque* ("secret meeting"), from Latin *colloquium* (English *colloquy*), possibly influenced by *dialogue*. Ultimately from Latin *collega* ("a partner in office") + Ancient

Greek **λόγος** (lógos, "speech; oration; discourse"), perhaps partly via Latin *loquor* ("I speak").

9. **Contumely**, from Old French *contumelie*, from Latin *contumēlia* ("insult"), perhaps from *com-* + *tumeō* ("swell").
10. **Coxcomb**, 17th century slang for a man overly concerned with his appearance
11. **Hullabaloo**, possibly a rhyming reduplication of *halloo* ("*used as a greeting or to catch attention; used in hunting to urge on pursuers*"), *hilloa, hullo* ("*variants of* hello"), and similar words.
12. **Crapulous**, caused by or showing the effects of alcohol. "I was a little too crapulous to register what had happened"
13. **Esurient**, late 17th century: from Latin *esurient-* 'being hungry', from the verb *esurire*, from *esse* 'eat'.
14. **Dandiprat** in C16: of unknown origin, English or dandyprat, archaic, a small boy or an insignificant person.
15. **Doxy**, dok'si, n. (Shak.) a mistress: a woman of loose character. [Prob. conn. with East Fries. dok, a bundle, Low. Ger. dokke. Dok'si, n. opinion—'Orthodoxy,' said Warburton, 'is my doxy—heterodoxy is another man's doxy.' [Gr. doxa, opinion.].
16. **Jade**, adultress, fornicatress, hussy, loose woman, slut, strumpet, trollop, a woman adulterer, jade.
17. **Gudgeon**, a fish or a person easily duped or cheated.

18. **Grimalkin**, noun, archaic, a cat or spiteful old woman!
19. **Fizgig**, fiz′gig, *n.* a giddy girl, a gadding, flirting girl. Also, a police informer.
20. **Gadzooks**, exclamation, archaic, an exclamation of surprise or annoyance.
21. **Gardyloo**, Interjection. (Scotland, obsolete) Used by people in medieval Scotland to warn passers-by of waste about to be thrown from a window into the street below. The term was still in use as late as the 1930s and 1940s, when many people had no indoor toilets.
22. **Lethophobia,** an abnormal anxiety of forgetting. Related 'sleep' units: dorm-; hypno-; narco-; oneiro- (dream); somni-; sopor-. Etymologically related 'forget, forgetfulness' word families: aletho-; oblivio-. Related 'memory, remember' word families: memor-; mne-.
23. **Malapert**, boldly disrespectful or insolent. **Moil**, drudgery or confusion or turmoil. **Mazed**, to be dazed or confused (or both).
24. **Periapt**, archaic, an item worn as a charm or amulet.
25. Quockerwodger (Noun) A wooden puppet controlled by strings. The term, although referring to a wooden toy figure which jerks its limbs about when pulled by a string, has been supplemented with a political meaning. A pseudo-politician, one whose strings of

action are pulled by somebody else, is now often termed a QUOCKERWODGER.

Usage: The shameless arts of the sycophant are not monopolised by Mr. Quocker-wodger and his congeners."

26. **Quothas**, archaic, *indeed, forsooth*.
27. **Rapscallion**, noun, archaic, humorous, *rascal, ne'er-do-well*.
28. **Scapegrace**, a mischievous or wayward person, especially a young person or child; a rascal.
29. **Shrive**, to hear confessions. to go to or make confession; confess one's sins, as to a priest. **Shrift**, absolution or remission of sins granted after confession and penance.
30. **Sluberdegullion**, slubber+ the British dialectal termgullion("wretch"). A filthy, slobbering person; a sloven, a villain, a fiend, a louse.
31. **Strumpet**, a female prostitute, a woman who has many casual sexual encounters or relationships.
32. **Turnkey** is a person who has charge of the keys of a prison; jailer. A **varlet** is a rascal or a page who serves a knight, or an attendant/servant.
33. **Moomin**, or Moomintroll, the main character in Tove Jansson's books and comic strips.
34. **Hierophant**, (ἱεροφάντης) is a person who brings religious congregants into the presence of that which

is deemed holy. As such, a hierophant is an interpreter of sacred mysteries and arcane principles.
35. **Unstilted** - flowing naturally and continuously; "unstilted conversation" unaffected - free of artificiality; sincere and genuine; "an unaffected grace".

Harry Matthews was born in rural Staffordshire, in 1980. After school in Shropshire, he read Philosophy and Politics at Reading University, graduating in 2002. In 2004 he wrote for the Amsterdam Weekly, after training in journalism, and pursued his passion for travel. In 2007 he started to write poetry, and in 2009 he started painting. He holds annual exhibitions of his paintings since 2012, and in the summer of 2020 wrote the poems that formed his first collections. He holds a Master of Arts degree in Writing from LJMU (2019).

Lightning Source UK Ltd.
Milton Keynes UK
UKHW010625100821
388609UK00001B/82